BULLDOOKEY

MILLARD EDWARD STREETER AND
PAMELA ELIZABETH SMITH

PAGE PUBLISHING
Conneaut Lake, PA

First originally published by Page Publishing 2024

ISBN 979-8-89157-415-1 (pbk)
ISBN 979-8-89157-424-3 (digital)

Printed in the United States of America

We dedicate this book in the loving memory
of Kareem Abdul Rahim Bey
November 10, 1953–September 2, 2023

CONTENTS

ACKNOWLEDGEMENTS

We say thank you to all who contributed to the development of *Bulldookey*. As you read through the pages of *Bulldookey*, you will recognize your contribution. There was a great cloud of contributors, many of you were strangers, and often this created duplications of ideas, thoughts, and considerations. Nonetheless, please, by all means, don't hesitate to pat yourselves on the back.

A special word of thanks to our families and friends, who put up with us as we plowed through creating this wonderful book and who had a tremendous impact in seeing this marvelous effort of love come to fruition.

It was a great pleasure to gather content from each and every one of you for the making of *Bulldookey*. It was a special pleasure to witness the eagerness you all had in sharing your thoughts and insights. We are eternally grateful for we could not have completed this work without your support.

We hope you enjoy reading *Bulldookey* as much as we enjoyed producing it. May all of you be blessed.

1. ***Can't wear white after Labor Day.*** Number one on the *Bulldookey* list was the very first item we discussed when *Bulldookey* was conceived. We had a good ole time laughing and tossing this nugget around. The concept was born in the early 1900s. Wearing white after Labor Day meant you were someone who had the means to have end-of-summer vacations. Only wealthy folks wore white after Labor Day. Wearing white after Labor Day was considered by some as wealthy people showing off. Some historians believed that this rule was a way for the wealthy to separate themselves from the working class. Not only could they afford vacations and the expensive clothes, but they didn't perform work that stained their white clothes. Lower-class working people wore dark clothing even in the summer to hide the dirt and grime that came with a hard day's work. In the twenty-first century, this fashion rule of the wealthy has been impaled because it is truly one of the stupidest rules devised by smart people. People wear colors of all varieties after Labor Day including white. Yay!

2. ***People who take kindness for weakness.*** This is just another sad commentary on the state of humankind. Kindness, the act of caring for another human being—shunned, my, my, my, preposterous! Words of encouragement, acts of helping another person randomly are frowned upon by some. Thoughtfulness and generosity smacked around by bullies are unappreciated. There is this perception that a kind person is soft and emotionally fragile while a person who is rude, ill-mannered, impolite, discourteous, uncivil, etc. is viewed as tough and someone to

be admired. This point of view is held up in our art, our music, our movies, and television shows. It is a real shame. We're "shaking our heads." Bulldookey! We prefer kindness.

3. ***People don't talk openly about aging/growing old in real talk/regular life***. It's a curious thing, but I notice that as I aged, people don't talk about aging in normal everyday life. No one we know talks about the experience of aging and the adaptations and adjustments that happen in the aging process. When I was younger, I remember hearing the older members of the group speak about arthritis, losing memory, losing hearing and sight, and other such things. But these things are not germane to aging (growing old). Young people can be affected by arthritis and loss of sight and hearing. They can even experience forgetfulness. My mother would say as she grew older, she was becoming forgetful. I would say to her, "Momma, what is my problem? I forget too." She would break forth with gleeful laughter.

I once said to my urologist, who is much older than me and who looked to be well past the age of retirement, "Doc, I notice that people don't talk about aging," and he responded, "I know and I am one of them." We both laughed. What I am referring to is the day-to-day journey, the everyday walk toward growing old, diet change if any, decrease of energy if any, change in sleep patterns if any, decrease in sexual energy if any, other physiological changes such as equilibrium imbalances (i.e. falling down), the affairs of the heart. Do we love more, or do we love less? Are we interested or disinterested in dating? What is maturation like from the ages of twenty to thirty to forty to fifty to sixty to seventy to eighty years of age? Why aren't we having real discussions concerning aging, especially in the sixty to seventy to eighty years ranges and beyond? Concerning the aging process, do we learn more or less as we age? What are the real benefits of growing old? What are the distractions and negative elements of aging?

As we age, I perceive we will have uniquely different experiences as well as shared and similar experiences. So let's be clear here, with the aging process, we are talking about those members of our society who are fifty years old and up—eighty, ninety, one hundred years of age. When I entered my sixties—somewhere around sixty-five—when I awakened in the night and got up out of bed, my balance/equilibrium was off, and I began falling down quite frequently; and it was frightening. This happening eventually improved, and I am not falling as once I had been. This could have been an adjustment period for me; I don't know. I'm just happy it has stopped for the time being. I never told my doctor about it. I was afraid. But I'll tell you this: I am glad for now it is over and yet I suspect it could return in my future.

One day as I was Ubering or Lyfting (ride-sharing), I met a young man in his thirties, and I told him of my observation of people not speaking openly and candidly about growing old. Well, this young man confided in me and said there was a time in his life when he was afraid/fearful/terrified of growing old. Are there others like this young man who are afraid of aging? Aging is a funny piece of work, downright hilarious on many levels and scary on others. As we honor life, we need more sensitivity toward our shared commonalities, more open communication, more trust, and honesty without fear. The business of aging ought to be in our daily life conversations, just as diet and leisure entertainment activities are in our 24-7.

4. ***Young people who do not respect their elders.*** This is a social tragedy, to put it mildly, and it is ancient in its origin. Young people disrespecting elder members of the group is a very serious matter. Many, many, many years ago, there was a group of children of the nation Israel who taunted an elderly man. Well, two she-bears came out of the forest and tore forty-two of them to pieces. You can read this account for yourselves. It is recorded in the Bible at 2 Kings 2:23–24. Yet the door swings both ways. Adults should not—because of their senior citizenship status—harass and exasperate children and young adults. This idea is also recorded in Bible and can be found at Colossians 3:21.

5. ***Life imitates art.*** This is a classic case of "which came first, the chicken or the egg?" Intelligence and intellectual, the pursuit of finding meaning in/to life is exhausting. To those proponents of the philosophy that life imitates art, what can I say? Mimesis or anti-mimesis? With all the knowledge and understanding the human race currently has at its disposal, we are merely scratching the surface. What we have learned is that some of us love to pontificate, be witty and clever, and stand on a soapbox, and we either buy or not buy what the speaker is offering. We spend hours upon hours searching for platforms from which others can hear our voice. Some of the stuff we come up with is spot-on; other stuff not spot-on. "Life imitates art" is in the not-spot-on category. With so many smart and intelligent people we have produced, for this one, we thought it best to look up the meaning of the word "life" in the dictionary. So to *Webster's Dictionary* we went. You know how this goes, there is a meaning one, meaning two, meaning three, meaning four, and so on, and so on—right? The truth is life is too big. We mean it is ultra-humongous. We could live forever, literally, and never totally discover all life's wonderful treasures.

    When I was a case manager conducting group sessions, I would put this question to the group, "What is life?" The answers were as varied and as many as those participants in the group. Then one day, a young man asked me this question. He said, "What do you say life is?" It was the first time I had ever been asked the question in a group session, so I paused to formulate my answer, and when I spoke, I said this, "Life is a complex system of things of which I am a part." Now I may be young, considering the age of the world and the universe and all the big heads that have come before me, but I really don't think there is an answer more sublime to the question, "What is life?" It is simple and it is accurate, and it is the undeniable truth. So Oscar Wilde, Plato, Socrates, Aristophanes, John Synge, James Joyce, romanticism versus idealism, phooey to you all! We say, let us all, everyone, get together and discuss what life is and how art fits into it, and we can include children in the discussion too.

6. ***Age is just a number***. Obviously, this is not true. Or maybe it is not obvious. Age is a number; this is for sure. But is it only just a number when it comes to evaluating the totality of a human being's existence? Only people who struggle with aging at any stage of the process adopt this mantra. A twelve-year-old may reason that age is just a number. A twenty-one-year-old may reason that age is just a number. A four-year-old may reason that age is just a number and so on and so on. Growing old or growing older seems to be troublesome for many people. In fact, history is not without evidence of this phenomena. For years, man has searched for a thing called "the fountain of youth." Even as I and my coauthor write this work, men and women (scientific researchers) all over the world are engaged in an investigation involving how to reverse the aging process. These scientists and researchers would even like to put an end to death and, in turn, do away with all sickness and disease that plague mankind. Some humans, nonetheless, have no need for delusional substitutions for accepting aging as a natural process of life. If you live, you will age. Unfortunately, there is a lot of nonsense floating around concerning aging coming from the professional to the novice, the hairdresser to the barber. The truth is growing old scares some people and, to some people, it does not. Age represents more than just its number.

7. ***You're only as old as you feel.*** This is another notion that is simply not true. If you are forty but you feel like twenty-one, are you twenty-one? Concerning my energy, I have a friend who says that I am like a two-year-old, and yet I am not two years old. It seems that artificial stimuli, data, and information has been dispensed into the world of mankind and some have digested these materials into their system, and it has affected their outlook, their viewpoint on youth and aging. Growing old is looked upon in a very discouraging manner by many. Yet there are some who are growing old graciously and gracefully. They are enjoying their aging process. People's energy is man-

aged by their personality coupled with their mind and spirit (energy), and we all have different personalities and levels of energy. This is what makes us unique. Fun-loving, outgoing, upbeat personalities do not experience the weighed down stress of aging, even when there is sickness associated with it. The experts do not know why, as we age, our cells—which should keep replenishing themselves and renewing themselves—at some point, simply stop renewing and reproducing. The body you had when you were born is not the body you have at sixteen. According to scientific researchers, this process of cell replacement or cell renewal should continue to infinity, but alas, it does not, and it drives scientists mad. "Why, why, why!" they pull out their hair and scream. And yet they continue to search for the answer and solution to aging. And we are not there yet, not even close.

8. ***Real men don't cry.*** We don't even know where to begin with this one. It is so ridiculous. Apparently, many of us lack an understanding of what it is to be human. We are not experts in the science of being human, but we are experts in the mundane. We know that our bodies have many systems and parts. For example, there is a system of organs—a musculoskeletal system, cardiovascular system, respiratory system, etc. You get my point.

This is from the National Eye Institute: Tears keep your eyes **wet and smooth** and help focus light so you can see clearly. They also protect your eyes from infections and irritating things, like dirt and dust. **Every time** you blink, a thin layer of tears called a "tear film" spread across the surface of your cornea—the clear outer layer of the eye. Tears come from glands above your eyes then drain into your tear ducts, small holes in the inner corners of your eyes, and down through your nose. When your eyes don't make enough tears or your tears don't work the right way, you can get dry eye.

What are tears made for? Tear film has three different layers: 1) The oily outer layer keeps tears from drying up too quickly and makes the surface of the eye smooth. 2) The watery middle layer keeps the eyes wet and nourishes the eye tissue. 3) The inner mucus layer helps the tear film stick to the surface of the eyes. Crying helps improve our mood.

Many people associate crying with sadness and making them feel worse. As a phenomenon unique to humans, crying is a natural response to a variety of emotions, from deep sadness and grief to extreme happiness and joy. Is crying good for you? The answer is a resounding yes! Thinkers and physicians of ancient Greece and Rome held the position that tears work as a purgative. Today's psychological thought agrees, emphasizing the role of crying as a means that allows us to release stress and emotional pain. Crying is not a sign of weakness or a lack of emotional fortitude. It is clear that "real men don't cry" is a load of crap.

9. ***Elbows off the table while eating.*** In my household this rule was punishable by law. When we researched this, there was just too much to shift through. From the origin of it being connected to sailors at sea using their elbows to keep their plates from sliding off the table to prisoners guarding their food from other prisoners. This social etiquette rule is so ridiculous we are not going to spend energy on this one. What we will say is elbows on the table is a really nice way to eat a nice piece of fried chicken leg or a delicious pork chop without some conscious social etiquette awareness of violating someone's personal space.

10. ***Girls are smarter than boys.*** Another piece of dung. Psychological reviews, this study, that study—it's all baloney! The genders are of equal intelligence. Born of equal intelligence. All in the DNA. My mother used to say to me, "Boy, you are too smart for you own britches." Man is too smart, at times, for his own britches. He will concoct all kinds of nonsense and go through great lengths and means to seek approval of these nonsenses. Example, the world is flat. We know that this is malarkey. But it was put out there for all of us to digest. This man is a composite man. And he changes with time. He loves confusion and controversy, and he is always at work.

11. ***No talking with food in your mouth***. Another social etiquette that is a load of *Bulldookey*. Eating and talking are the most natural of human behaviors. A good meal has been prepared. It is time to eat. You are not eating alone. There are others, family and friends. The most boring meal is a silent one. There should be conversations during meals. Lighthearted and hearty conversations. Pompousness should never be on display during eating time. This is the time for letting down your hair. For enjoying your company and the delicious food prepared by the cook. Let's eat, let's talk.

12. ***Men earn more money than women***. For years I was stumped by this factoid. The gender pay gap—the difference between the earnings of men and women—has barely closed in the United States in the past two decades, according to the Pew Research Center. In a world where I exist, this simply wasn't true. To this day, in every job I have ever held my female counterpart made exactly the same pay or salary that I made. Then where does this fact come from, and to whom does it pertain? Well, interestingly enough, it comes from corporate America. Apparently in corporate America, a male vice president of operations is paid a higher salary than his female associate performing the same job classification. Incredulous! Right! Why? According to the Pew Research Center, in 2022, American women typically earned eighty-two cents for every dollar earned by men. This is just embarrassing.

13. ***Women are treated as less than by men/society/social structures/etc.*** While this social stigma—women being held in less esteem than men—has changed over the years, yet some still subscribe to the old adage to keep them "barefoot and pregnant." For centuries, women have been considered as second-class citizens. And they still are in some parts of the world. It wasn't until 1920 that women in the United States won the right to vote. This sacrilegious, unconscionable position of perceiving women as lower than men still exists. There are men who still mistreat our womenfolk. They are extremely abusive, verbally, physically, and spiritually, and our court system is

inundated with domestic violation cases. A woman's life is no less important than a man's. In fact, the value of each—male and female—is equally the same. In some cases, the male is physically stronger, but so what? This fact does not make his life more valuable than his female counterpart. A man cannot bear children. Yet the fact that a woman can have babies does not make her more valuable than her male counterpart.

14. ***Black don't crack.*** We have got to give this one a black eye. It is time that black don't crack to be completely knocked out. This entry was given to me by my very lovely and beautiful daughter. She was forty-two years old at the time when she said to put this on the *Bulldookey* list. As we discussed this one, we were not sure if we wanted to include it on the *Bulldookey* list. Because this concept is so sacred in the African American community. Black don't crack is like the Ten Commandments, it's on Mount Rushmore, it is like the very Word of God to many African Americans. But upon continued ponderance, we decided that it was indeed eligible to be one of the shining stars of our *Bulldookey* list. Black don't crack is absolutely and ridiculously dumb and untrue. My daughter was emphatic when she said, "Daddy, that's not true."

So why do African Americans revere this nonsense? As best we can tell, it has something to do with their White counterpart. When it comes to aging, it is believed that White people wrinkle way faster than Blacks. They (White people) develop lines in their skin on the outer corners of their eyes. These are lateral canthal lines known as crow's feet. Well, the truth is Blacks develop the same physiological deterioration of their skin as Caucasians. It has nothing to do with race. In fact, it may just be an individual thing. A seventy-year-old White man could possibly look better than a sixty-year-old Black man. And a sixty-year-old Black woman could look worse than a seventy-year-old White woman. Kiely Williams—an American singer, dancer, and actress—is on record, stating she resents the people who told her that black don't' crack. She said, "I cracked like Pookie from *New Jack City*." Biologically, the whole science of this is too intense for this space, but the notion that black don't crack is simply not true. Black does crack!

15. ***Everything happens for a reason.*** For those who subscribe to this edit, we are just shaking our heads. As a principle, we find it wanting. The problem begins with the word "everything" and the word "reason." Here are a few questions for all those who expound on this maxim: What is the reason to the child who has been sexually violated by an adult? Or what is the reason to the innocent man found guilty of a crime he did not commit? Or the reason to a woman constantly battered by her mate? We rest here. There are just too many examples to cite. We are sure that those who promote this nonsensical hogwash has an answer that sounds good to them.

16. ***What doesn't kill you only makes you stronger.*** Who are we kidding with this one? We don't even want to repeat it; it is so ridiculous. You see the thing about principles of this nature, they have to be applicable across the board. It has to be able to be applied in all areas of contemplation.

    Here is a synopsis: A man went to war? He came out of the war emotionally and mentally damaged. He lost one arm and one leg. He did not die. How does his result make him stronger? In what way and by what means is he stronger than he was before entering the war? Now we are not saying that there aren't experiences we might have that are traumatic and painful, and as a result of having had these experiences, we emerge from them strengthened. Recovering from a nasty divorce comes to mind. Having one's heart broken may be another such instance where an individual may emerge stronger than they were before. It's obvious that things such as these are not necessarily going to kill us. And we come out of them stronger and feeling fit. And, too, the addict and alcoholic that gets clean and sober from things that clearly can kill you, and they still survive. They don't die. In these types of situations and circumstances, it could be said, "What doesn't kill you only makes you stronger." But as a principle, it fails to meet every possible scenario where death can be imminent and the person rise out of the circumstance stronger.

17. ***God watches out for babies and fools.*** What is this all about? Well, we tried to find the source of this expression, and we were not able to. There are certain biblical references that some refer to such as Palms 116:6, which, according to The Living Bible, says, "The Lord protects the simple and the childlike…" Well, this is a far cry from babies and fools. It would seem to me that God would leave the fool to his own devices. Here are three things the Bible says about the fool or stupid ones: 1) A fool hates his mother (Proverbs 15:20); 2) A fool makes light of sin (Proverbs 10:23); 3) A fool only trusts his own counsel (Proverbs 28:26). Now we ask you, Why would God be looking out for these folks? This group of people wouldn't even merit the Creator's attention. "Do not pray in behalf of this people…for I will not listen" (Jeremiah 7:16). Some people like to say things that they think are clever and profound when in truth the thing said is really foolishness. As for the babies, we could find nothing in the Bible stating God looks out for them.

18. ***Every cloud has a silver lining.*** This is hogwash at the highest level. And it is considered a proverb? It reflects a notion that no matter how bleak a situation (might seem), there is (always) some good aspect to be discerned. We are not going to spend a lot of time here. It is clear that for some living in bad situations, things never improve—they never get better. In fact, in some of these situations, matters become worse. Presenting people with a false sense of anything is just plain cruel and criminal. But cruelty seems to be the calling card for many of us humans.

19. ***"Everybody plays the fool; there is no exception to the rule,"*** a song by Main Ingredient. Beautiful song, but is it true? What we found to be true in our limited time on earth is that everyone is limited by their own experiences. And we make the errant conclusion of thinking that everyone else in the world experiences the same things we do. How many of you have actually played the fool? Raise your hands. Higher! Just joking, you can put your hands down.

20. ***Learning to love yourself is the greatest love of all***. Whoever coined this phrase was on drugs. The greatest love of all is to love God with all your heart and with all your soul and with all you mind. No love is greater than this!

21. ***Step on a crack, break your mama's back***. How many cracks must I step on? If you had a bad mother, this sentiment would certainly have gone a long way in remedying the situation. And if you currently have a mother from Hades, keep stepping on those cracks. Now if you have a dear, sweet, nurturing mother, avoid the cracks at all costs.

22. ***Don't put your hat on the bed***. This is one of the greatest superstitions of all time and exists in many cultures. It means it is bad luck to put your hat on a bed. There existed a notion that not putting a hat on a bed prevented the spread of head lice. Another is connected to the 1920s, when gangsters hid guns in their hats on beds in hotel rooms. But here is the most popular rendition of the superstition, evil spirits lived in your hair, so by putting your hat on the bed where your head goes, the evil spirits spilled out. Why do we have a propensity to create such nonsense? And then proceed to live by them! No wonder many of us are in therapy and never get well.

23. ***Don't walk under a ladder***. This superstition originates in Christendom. The triangular shape form by leaning the ladder against the wall resembles the Holy Trinity. It is believed that to pass underneath this triangle would be a violation of God's space and would incur his wrath. You have got to be kidding. What reasonably intelligent person would succumb to such balderdash?

24. ***Black cat crossing in front of you***. The superstitions associated with a black cat crossing your path are one of the oldest and most well-known superstitions. The meaning varies from culture to culture. For example, in the UK, Ireland, and Germany, the black cat crossing your path from left to right is considered to bring you good luck. There is also this belief held by gamblers in Las Vegas that if a black cat crosses them while they are on their way to the casino—either driving or walking—it will

bring them bad luck, and they shouldn't gamble that night. And so they don't. Hmmm, could have hit the jackpot on that day!

25. ***No such thing as a free lunch***. "No such thing as a free lunch" is an idiom used to convey the idea that it is not possible to get something that is desired or valuable without having to pay for it in some way. It assumes that things appearing free always have some cost paid by somebody, or that nothing in life is free. What do you think? Do you believe in this *Bulldookey?* There are so many things that are absolutely free in life; we don't know what to cite first. Let's start with the most obvious thing that is free in life—air! Believe us if some greedy business entity could find a way to make the occupants of earth pay for air, they would.

Stop the music! Some greedy businesspeople are already selling air. The product is called "oxygen bar" and retails for up to $499. Oxygen bars are found in malls, casinos, and nightclubs. These "bars" serve purified oxygen, often infused with scents. Proponents of recreational oxygen therapy claim that hits of purified oxygen boost energy levels, relieve stress, and cure hangovers, but there is no evidence to support these claims. Though water has been commercialized, there was a time when it was free. How about friendship? What does it cost? And love, do you really pay for it? Let's get crude for a moment. The foregoing observation is not offered to offend anyone. Take the matter of sex, taboo, right? Well, it might surprise you that a woman does not necessarily have to give a man her sex just to get a dollar. There are men who will freely give a woman money with the absence of sex. What kind of shit is that? Hard to believe, right? Well, it is true. Do your own personal investigation, survey some women you know, and you will discover that many of them, or a few of them, one of them, have male friends who would give them money from time to time with no expectation of sex in return as payment for their grandiose deed. This might be a rare phenomenon, but I can personally attest that it is true. The truth is there are things in life that are free and cost absolutely nothing!

26. ***Nothing in life is free***. This is just a variation to the theme. Nothing else to say here, right? Except *Bulldookey*!

27. ***Life isn't fair***. This one is an all-time classic and perhaps the toughest to mine through on this list because it involves every single individual on this planet. Of course, this is a perspective, perception issue. To address this idiom properly, we think a question needs to be asked first. And that question is, What is life? For centuries, we have been attempting to answer this question. And the answers to it are exhaustive. So I came up with an answer that I think should satisfy every seeker of the answer. Here it is. You first were introduced to the meaning of life in item number five on the *Bulldookey* list. Life is a complex system of things of which I am a part of. There is the solar system, the nervous system, respiratory system, cardiovascular system—a plethora of systems that make up life. For us, the issue is to be able to distinguish between what life is and circumstances, events, happenings, and things of those sorts as we contemplate what life is. Someone robs you at gunpoint. Is this life being unfair, or is it an event taking place in life? A student takes a test and fails. Is this an example of life being unfair? Or is it a consequence of someone's own action? Two nations go to war, is it life's fault? We beg to differ. When I look at life without people in the picture, life looks pretty awesome. I mean absolutely beautiful. Try it. But when you factor in people, what we consider life has a different appearance. So it isn't life that is unfair; it is people that are not fair. And life gets blamed!

28. ***A dog is a man's best friend***. Well now, this is just ridiculous. I have had a couple of dogs, and I would never go as far as to say they were my best friends. People who place a sentimental value on their relationship with their pet(s) at a greater value than relationships with other humans, we just don't know what to say. It is a personal matter, we guess!

29. ***But for the grace of God, there go I***. There are different variations to this theme. However old this proverbial saying is and

no matter who first coined it, it is utterly offensive on so many levels. It is a Christian saying meant as a statement of humility and gratitude toward God for the blessings one has received versus a less fortunate soul. That this would be the Christian God's perspective is unthinkable. What accounts for one person faring better in life than another person could have absolutely nothing to do with God. But because God is God, some people like to attribute every single thing that happens on this earth to him. Here is a scripture for you: "When under trial (the person who is in a less fortunate situation than you), let no one say, 'I am being tried by God.' For with evil things God cannot be tried (accused of) nor does he himself try anyone" – James 1:13. Here is another thought for those Christians who subscribe to this lame proverb that comes from their God and also contained in the Bible: "In every nation, he that fears him and does what is right is acceptable to him" – Acts 10:35. And again in the Bible: "There is neither Jew nor Greek, there is neither slave nor freeman, there is neither male nor female, for you are all one in union with Christ Jesus" – Galatians 3:28. Now to bring this puppy to a close, read for yourselves Acts 10:34. Drop the mike! How dare you look down on another person's unfortunate situation and imagine that you have been favored by God more than that individual? Drop the mike twice! *Boom, boom.*

30.   ***I'm just not myself.*** Then who in the world are you? We have heard people say this, and it has always befuddled us. If I get angry and lash out at someone, is it not still me? If I am sick and feeling miserable, is it not still me? If I get caught up with the wrong crowd and break the law, it is still me. Everything I do is me. Everything you do is you. Why we have a tendency toward making excuses; pretending and falsifying who and what we are defies our understanding. There are only a few things in life better than embracing who you are completely. Our personality and character will go through changes. But in every experience we have in life, we are who we are. We are never not ourselves. And we know someone will say, "You know what I mean." And we will say, "We do not."

31. ***It wasn't me (the guilty man's anthem)***. This is funny, right? Everyone is innocent. No one is guilty. Well, somebody did it! What do you think?

32. ***Don't put off until tomorrow what you can do today***. Another classic that needs further ponderance, which is really whacky. First it begs the question, Why not? Why not put off until tomorrow something that you can do today? Putting things off until tomorrow makes all the sense in the world. Imagine if you attempted to cram every single thing you could possibly do all in one day, you would be exhausted every day and driving yourself to an early death. You may want to wash and dry your clothes today and, tomorrow, fold them up and put them away. Even though you could fold and put the clothes away today, there is no reason why you couldn't wait until tomorrow. It's okay and perfectly all right to do; don't kill yourself prematurely. Tomorrow presents itself with a multitude of possibilities and opportunities that are present today. So what? It is nice to look forward to tomorrow. Up next?

33. ***Tomorrow isn't promised to you***. This one is very tricky. When I began considering this one, the first thing for me is the word "promise." In order for there to be no promise of tomorrow, there must be a possibility of a promise, a source who would be able to make or not make the promise. After this consideration, I asked, Who could the author of such a non-promise or promise be? And secondly, this source would have to also be in control of tomorrow, right? For you can only promise what you personally control and own. Now we have the nuts and bolts of the matter. We have a non-promise centering on tomorrow. Here is what I was able to piece together. I went back to the days of my father. Then I went back to the days of my father's father and then his father. What I discovered is this, tomorrow continued to show up throughout each man's lifetime and continued to come even into my own lifetime. In fact, tomorrow never ceased to show up. Interesting, right? Because tomorrow never ceases to arrive; it comes as if it is promised. Here is the owner of the promise and the keeper of tomorrow speaking,

"From now on, the earth will never cease to have seed sowing and harvest, cold and heat, summer and winter, and day and night" – Genesis 8:22. So from our perspective, it would seem that tomorrow is promised to each and every one of us. Another question before we leave—Why do *we* fail to experience each and every tomorrow? It is not tomorrow's fault; tomorrow continues to fulfill the promise. Look, it came today!

34. ***Making men put the toilet seat down.*** Hmmm, this one will break up a relationship, depending on how strictly the rule is enforced. Toilet seat up, toilet seat down, each member of the household should be held equally responsible to survey the bathroom when they enter it. The reason for this is that we are not perfect. Of course, it is known that it is the man or men leaving the toilet seat up. Yet when the men or women of the household go into the bathroom knowing they have to sit on the toilet seat, they should pay attention to see if the toilet seat is up or down. There should be a shared responsibility here. I have fallen in the toilet a few times when I was not the one who left the toilet seat up. It doesn't matter who left the toilet seat up, I failed to survey the bathroom. Now for us guys, when you are using the toilet for urination and the toilet seat is down and you squirt pee on the toilet seat, clean up your mess. It is just that simple. Now the toilet seat stays down. Yet don't forget you must survey the bathroom when you enter to determine if the toilet seat is up or down.

35. ***Love is strange.*** We have absolutely no idea what this means. Time and time again, "love is strange" shows up in songs, theaters, and movies as a theme. As recently as 2014, there was a release of a film braving this title *Love Is Strange*, starring Alfred Molina, John Lithgow, and Marisa Tomei. What we have found is that God and love are the two most abused and misused words in our universe. Here is how it works for us: God is love and love is God. We seem to be all over the place with our interpretation and understanding on love's meaning. One of the most disturbing renderings of love's character is this: someone who loves in his/her own way. What is this?

Usually, this kind of love is associated with emotional, mental, physical, and spiritual abuse. Who needs this kind of love? If anyone ever says to you, "I love you in my own way," run for your life! Do not stay.

36. ***Love is a battlefield.*** This made the list, and we were going to make comments, then we decided not to. It is a concept offered in a song by singer Pat Benatar in 1983. It was considered by some as one of the greatest songs of the '80s. Again, this must be a perspective thing because it is obvious to us that love is absolutely not a battlefield. But the song made a lot of money and no doubt influenced a lot of people.

37. ***Love makes you do crazy things.*** Here is some more stupidity. It is not love making us do crazy things. It is our mismanagement of energy (love), and we blame love for our abnormal thinking and behavior. We say love made me do it. You bust out someone's window and then run because you want to get their attention. Love made you do it? You stalk someone for days, weeks, months. Love made you do it? Love gets blamed for our wacky behaviors when it is not love that is responsible, but rather, our inability to manage ourselves ethically, morally, correctly. WE must blame ourselves, not love. One word for all of us acting in this manner—STOP!

38. ***Jesus born on the twenty-fifth of December***. Everyone on earth knows that this a load of crock. In fact, Jesus' birth date isn't even known. The early Christian Church did not celebrate Jesus' birthday. But this space is not the space for the debate. Suffice it to say, everyone knows Jesus wasn't born on December 25. Even if Jesus was born on December 25, his birthday celebration is the weirdest, strangest birthday celebration we have ever witnessed in our lives. Jesus is the only person we know who, on his birthday, doesn't receive not one gift! Not one! Let us put it this way—we have never seen anyone give the birthday man a gift. No gift under the famed Christmas tree. Have you? Strange, right? *Bulldookey*!

39. ***Santa Claus.*** This *Bulldookey* ruined my life. For years on Christmas Eve, I stared up into the sky, looking for what? The

famous mythical Santa Claus. He was very illusive, this guy. I mean this dude was extremely good because in all those years of looking into the sky on Christmas Eve for Santa Claus, I never saw him. Have any of you? Even until this day, I continue to have trust issues. Laugh out loud!

40. ***Krampus.*** Krampus is really a load of *Bulldookey.* He is a horned anthropomorphic creature in the Central and Eastern Alpine folklore of Europe, who during Advent Season, scares children who misbehave. Assisting Santa Claus, the pair visit children on the night of December 6, rewarding well-behaved children with gifts and badly behaved children with punishment from Krampus. What loving, intelligent human being would create such nonsense? You tell us. Why man seems to have a rich appetite for this useless kind of blarney is beyond me.

41. ***Flying reindeer.*** Stop with this nonsense already. Cease and desist. Everyone continuing to perpetuate the nonsense of Santa and his flying reindeers ought to be arrested, tried for fraud, and imprisoned. Enough said.

42. ***Easter Bunny.*** Are you kidding us? This guy is still roaming the earth!

43. ***Tooth Fairy.*** And this one, you have got to be kidding me! Do you know how many teeth I put under my pillow and received nothing. Nothing! And I know I am not the only one living with this humongous disappointment, right?

44. ***Scientists have figured out how and when our sun will die.*** According to a study in the journal *Nature Astronomy*, the sun will die in ten million years. We don't know what you think about this, but it is entirely too heavy for us. While there is something to be said about the accomplishments of science, we are more creationists. "From now on, the earth will never cease, having seed sowing and harvest, cold and heat, summer and winter, day and night" (Genesis 8:22). No, no, no, the sun will never, never, never die!

45. ***Youth is wasted on the young.*** Why would youth be wasted on the young when it is especially for the young? This con-

cept is attributed to Irish writer George Barnard Shaw, who expressed his disdain for the lack of appreciation and intelligence of young people. Perhaps Mr. Shaw had forgotten that he himself was once young. It also implies that young people do not make the best use of their time and energy. We do not know how old Mr. Shaw was when he made this ridiculous comment, but was he mistaken? Old people need to just stop and behave themselves. We have heard of old people who have forgotten what it is like to be young, and they turn resentful and bitter toward young people. Youth is spent exactly as it should be. What hogwash!

46. ***Kill them with kindness***. This made our list, but we are not going to spend a lot of time on this. The concern for us is the word "kill." Plain and simple. It just doesn't make any sense no matter how many people use it to make the point; instead of returning insult or rudeness with insult or rudeness, use kindness. Personally, for this idiom to work for us, we need to see some actual dying.

47. ***Love hurts***. This made our list, and it should have been grouped with numbers thirty-five, thirty-six, and thirty-seven. Love has never hurt anyone in its life. People hurt and then they blame love. Not fair. Why not say, "That motherfucker hurt me."

48. ***Deliberate mistake***. Here we go! The concept of deliberately making mistakes is entirely based on the fact that we learn from our mistakes. So when we commit a mistake willingly (what?), then it is clear that if we fail, we are going to learn some lesson from that failure and try not to repeat the same. But if we succeed, the mistake results in innovation and better opportunities. You have got to be blowing our socks off! Who makes a mistake deliberately to learn some lesson if, indeed, you already know that what you are doing is a mistake? Who does this? The examples to the folly of this concept are like the stars in the sky.

49. ***Honest thief***. Really? What is wrong with our sense of values? *Honest Thief* is a 2020 movie starring Liam Neeson, an iconic actor. Every adult in the world probably has seen one of Mr. Neeson's films. Why do we have a need to twist perceptions,

make right wrong and wrong right? Call a lie a little lie or fib—no big thing. And then beg for and require truth and honesty from among the members of our society. Really?

50. ***Organized chaos***. Again, faulty perception at its worst. What kind of tomfoolery is this? Organized chaos is described as a situation where there is a lot of confusion and no organization, which surprises you that the results are good. Hmmm. In all these types of instances of apparent confusion and mass hysteria, there is always someone or several *someones* deflecting and taking control, thus producing your favorable outcome. I have been in a few of these environments, and it has been said of me that I am a solution man. Chaos is never organized. Here is the meaning of chaos—complete disorder and confusion. Clearly a situation like this needs someone to take control. Chaos lacks the ability to organize itself. What say you?

51. ***Ride or die.*** There are a lot of fans of this urban concept. And it is very controversial. This term was born out of hip-hop music and culture. Its earliest reference was from female rappers declaring their loyalty to their partners who lived dangerous lifestyles. I guess this concept is broke for me because, first of all, as a parent, you want to raise decent human beings. You want your children to be honest and honorable. All right, we know we all are not on the same page. Things can go sideways for our children even when we have done the very best we can do for them. But to be willing to give up your precious life for some *Bulldookey* concept such as "ride or die," hmmm…we don't know about that. We know we live in a world where there is little, or no, value shown for life. But here's the thing, bad influences need to be eradicated. Not died for! Who's with us?

52. ***Let's agree to disagree***. Another fan favorite. I tested this on several people as they rode in my vehicle as I did Lyft and Uber transportation services. This principle has so many holes in it, it is like Swiss cheese. As a principle, it fails across the board. It does not meet the test such as the principle "safety first." Safety can be applied in every area of our lives. Safety first highly recommends that we be careful in everything that we do. Let's

agree to disagree does not measure up to the test for all areas of our lives. It only works for things of little impact or consequences. For example, you say I like mustard; I say mustard is nasty, then you say it is the best; I say you must be crazy because mustard is the nastiest of all the condiments. You say, "Let's agree to disagree." Okay, no harm, no foul. Nobody is hurt. Now try this on for size. Someone burglarizes your house. He carries out his deed. He gets caught. When you are allowed to confront him about his behavior and attempt to explain to him the error of his ways, he says to you, "Let's agree to disagree." Do you see the issue this principle creates? As long as we agree to disagree on issues of importance and come to no resolve, we are always going to be under threat and suspicion and have a lack in our sense of security. A thief cannot say to us, "Let's agree to disagree." What? Someone here has clearly lost their mind. Now someone may think this saying is clever, hip, and slick, but as a principle that can be applied across the board, it is ridiculous. It simply does not work.

53. ***OMG.*** God has been reduced to a cliché. It's OMG this and OMG that. You get a hangnail (OMG). Drop food on the floor (OMG). Hit your shinbone (OMG). It's raining (OMG). See something funny (OMG). If this is a generic god, it doesn't matter. But if the god implied in OMG is the God of the Holy Scriptures, God Almighty, the Creator, then it really matters. This is what it says in Exodus 20:7: "You must not take the name of God in vain (or worthless way) for God will not hold him guiltless that takes up his name in a worthless way." You see, the name of God is a pretty big thing to him. Now, it may not be as big a of thing to those who go around saying, "OMG this" and "OMG that," but it is a big deal to the owner of the name, namely God!

54. ***Children should be seen and not heard.*** What a poor way to develop a child. As adults, we all know that children need training. Training and upbringing are vital to maturation. This expression means that children should be respectful and behave around adults. It also means that children should speak

only when an adult speaks to them. The expression is a way of describing proper behavior in children belonging to strict parents. I am shivering. I make no bones that the Bible is my favorite book of all. And here is an idea conveyed in it: "Fathers, do not exasperate your children" – Colossians 3:21. I think many parents and adults struggle with the application of this instruction. It is truly amazing that some of us turn out not so bad after being raised by a parent or parents who stifled our development, both emotionally and intellectually, with a strict adherence to this rule. Other children who move into adulthood are not so fortunate.

55. ***Women belong in the kitchen.*** This is just downright disrespectful. Whatever culture this concept was derived from or originated from performed a mighty disservice to our womenfolk. The principles of respect, decency, intelligence, kindness, thoughtfulness, generosity, meekness, love, compassion, loyalty, etc., etc., etc., etc. should always be afforded and extended in their behalf. What kind of man is the man—and we know it was a man who first said this—would say such an unkind, unflattering thing out of his face? What woman would remain with such a man?

56. ***Women should be barefoot and pregnant.*** We wanted to include this on the *Bulldookey* list because this expression also had a lot of fire and continues to burn to this today.

57. ***Serve black-eyed peas for New Year's Day.*** It will bring your house good luck. Black-eyed peas on January 1 will bring you a year worth of prosperity. But luck won't stick, according to many legends, if you don't eat them with greens (which symbolize money), cornbread (which symbolizes gold), and pork (which symbolizes luck). How well is this superstition doing? Well, a lot of people follow this tradition. And they have not prospered! But we still eat black-eyed peas every January 1 because they simply taste good.

58. ***Don't split the pole; it brings bad luck.*** Splitting the pole is considered bad luck by some people. When walking in a group and obstructed by an obstacle, a pole, a traffic cone, whatever

it may be, it is important that the group not separate on either side of the obstacle. Because if they do, the most unfortunate things are going to happen to them all.

59. ***The customer is always right.*** Well, what can we give you all on this piece of gem? First two questions are in order: Is this true? Is the customer always right? No, it is not true. No, the customer is not always right. One Sunday afternoon, we were in the market shopping. I observed three elderly people, two women and a man all dressed up, looking as if they had attended church that day, or they were on their way to church. They were at the eggs section. As I watched, it became clear to me that they were switching eggs from one egg carton to another egg carton, perhaps moving extra-large eggs into the small eggs cartons. Two of them were posted up so as to give cover to the one who was switching the eggs. As I watched them, I started laughing. What I was witnessing was so hilarious. I mean, from appearance these folks, really looked like they had just left church or were on their way to church. I called my significant other over so she could watch with me. We both cried with laughter. Several years ago, I purchased a TV from Walmart. I took the TV home and broke it while taking it out of the box. I was miffed. I took the TV back to Walmart and told a lie. Walmart returned my money to me, and I purchased another TV. Was the customer right? The customer is only right when the customer is right. When the customer is wrong, the customer is wrong.

60. ***Eat the burnt, it will make you pretty.*** My mother would tell me this whenever she burned her food, which was extremely rare. My mother was the best cook on earth. But when she would occasionally burn something, she would say, "Eat the burnt, it will make you pretty." And I believed her. She was my mother. I never got pretty! *Bulldookey!*

61. ***A bump on your tongue means you are lying.*** When this one was given to me by a friend, I have to admit, I had never heard of it before. And if I had, I certainly had forgotten it. Lie bumps, also known as transient lingual papillitis, are small

red or white bumps that occur on the tongue and cause discomfort. They are called lie bumps because of a myth that the bumps appear on a person's tongue when they told a lie. The exact cause of lie bumps is unknown.

62.   ***You can't have your cake and eat it too***. My son said, "I got some *Bulldookey* for you, Pop."

I said, "What you got?"

He said, "You can't have your cake and eat it too. Why not? It makes more sense to slice a slice of cake and then eat it."

For as much reason and sense that is applied to this proverb, like my son, it makes me scratch my head and stick my thumb in my mouth. This proverb literally means you cannot simultaneously retain your cake and eat it. What? Who wants to have his cake just to have it, sitting there, watching it, watching it, watching it, watching it because you can't have it and eat it too. It is used to say that there are two options that someone wants but can't have both because the options conflict with each other, so they can only pick one. Even with this perspective, the idiom—having the cake and not eating it—is not closely congruent. In the matter of choice, there is no conflict in the decision-making process—I want cake, I want to eat cake; this is completely logical. In addition, it is also used to remind someone that they have to decide, and that decision is going to result in something negative. No matter which option someone chooses, they are going to miss out on the other. Hmmm, make sense… I don't know. Example, going to college or going to work? Either way, you are going to miss out on the pleasures provided by the unselected choice. I am still not convinced that having your cake and not eating it adequately represents this situation. People have gone to college and worked full-time jobs. Now let's see if we can make this conundrum work. Somewhere along life's line, I heard a better interpretation of the proverb. Have you ever heard the one about a story being passed down and down and down and down until the original story is distorted and lost? Well, here is the story I heard: There was a man who was conflicted and tormented. He was seeing two women. One woman's name was Kate, and the other woman's name was Edith. This man spoke to a friend about his dilemma, and the friend said, "You can't have Kate and Edith too."

63. ***Racial and ethnic slurs***. What can we say about the poor behaviors and mental dispositions of others? Mean-spiritedness, hatred, envy, jealousy, unfounded suspicion are human characteristics that must be crushed and abolished. But this behavior speaks to something deeper about the human condition. What is that you might ask? This is not the place for that consideration.

64. ***Never talk religion or politics***. Religion and politics are the two main systems of every society and culture. It is impossible not to talk about them. Yes, we could refrain from doing so, but why? Oh, that's right, people have a propensity to not control themselves; we lack self-control and begin to quarrel when it comes to these two subjects. Not all humans lack self-control, but the vast majority of us lose our minds on these two very important and vital matters. Something is amiss hear.

65. ***Don't put all your eggs in one basket***. My son said to me again, "Pop, I got another one for you."

And I said, "What you got?"

Then he said, "Don't put all your eggs in one basket. This is some *Bulldookey*. Why not?"

The meaning behind this idiom is you should not risk everything or depend entirely on a single thing or course of action. It advises against investing all your resources, time, or efforts in a single venture as it leaves you vulnerable to failure and loss. While there is something to be said in support of this proverb, does it apply across the board in all facets of our choosing and decision-making? When a woman decides to get married to one man, isn't she putting all the eggs in one basket? And resting her hopes and dreams on the one basket she has chosen? We mean that she could remain single and distribute her eggs between many baskets. And vice versa for the man.

66. ***Don't spend all your money in one place***. Here comes that son of mine again. "Pop," he said, "I got another piece of *Bulldookey* for you."

I said, "What you got?"

He said, "Don't spend all your money in one place."

I asked him, "Why is this *Bulldookey*?"

He said, "First of all, whoever is saying this should mind their own business. People should not have their eyes on other people's money."

As a proverb, "Don't spend all your money in one place" falls short of being the best advice. Everyone's economic situation is different. Example, a woman is behind in her rent. She plays the lottery and wins. The amount of winnings is equivalent to what she needs to catch up the rent. She tells a friend about her good fortune, and the friend says, "Don't spend it all in one place." But the woman does exactly that; she spends all the money she won playing the lottery on her rent. She spent all the money she won on the lottery in one place. Some people, because of their circumstances, feel as though they must rob Peter to pay Paul.

67. ***Sticks and stones may break my bones, but words will never hurt me***. Everyone should know that this is a great, big load of crock. Words hurt! We feel no example is warranted here. Even the thickest of skin can be penetrated. For some reason, people don't like to admit to vulnerability. People want to be hard. We don't want to admit to being sensitive. So we pretend that we are not injured, we are not hurt when someone insults us. In fact, someone coined the phrase, "Hit me with your best shot" and "Is that all you got?" suggesting that they want more. Ludicrous!

68. ***Boys will be boys***. This is *Bulldookey* on a very grand scale. Nothing really needs to be said here. It is a complete waste of energy. Boys will be boys, girls will be girls, men will be men, women will be women, cats will be cats, dogs will be dogs, rain will be rain, snow will be snow, cheese will be cheese, toast will be toast, and so on and so on and so on. But when

an expression like "boys will be boys" is used to excuse poor behavior or disruptive tendencies, then clearly, we have a problem. Wouldn't you say?

69. ***Beauty is only skin deep***. "Beauty is Only Skin Deep" is a song recorded by a R&B group, The Temptations in the '60s. But is it true? If it is true, what is to be said for beauty that isn't skin deep, that isn't way down beneath the surface of the skin deep, deep inside? The beauty that is on the top, on the surface, is this beauty not beauty because it is not below the skin but on the surface of the skin and can be readily seen by all witnessing eyes? Wait a minute, this kind of beauty can't exist. Why? Because beauty **is only** skin deep.

70. ***Break a mirror, seven years of bad luck***. Another idiotic precept. For man to be so intelligent, it is amazing how we make up and get caught up in all kinds of irrational thoughts and behaviors. The mirror superstition perhaps developed from when we first saw our reflection in the water. A belief developed that the image in the water was our actual soul and to endanger it would mean causing danger to our other self, the one producing the reflective image. It was also believed that mirrors had magical powers, "Mirror, mirror on the wall, who's the fairest of us all?" It was also believed that mirrors had the power to see the future and were the devices of the gods. So breaking a mirror would take away the mirror's power, and the soul of the person breaking the mirror would be detached from the body and misfortune would befall the one whose image was last seen by the mirror. But it is the Romans who are credited with coining the phase to break a mirror would bring you seven years of bad luck. The time, seven years came from a Roman belief that it took seven years for life to renew itself. At the end of the seven years of bad luck, your life would be renewed, and your life would be physically rejuvenated and the curse lifted. We think that there are people who still believe this *Bulldookey*.

71. ***The bigger they are, the harder they fall***. This idiom is used to assert that the more important or powerful a person is, the more difficult it is for them when they lose their power or

importance. The phrase is believed to have come from boxing and gained steam when boxer Robert Fitzsimmons said it in a 1902 newspaper article before fighting the much heavier James J. Jefferies. The proverb means that those who are physically large, powerful, or influential will have more to lose when they fail. First this concept is really about physical bigness and nothing more. The secondary stuff, power, and influence are add-ons from later developments or expansions of the original concept. But even when we factor in those added perspectives, those added ingredients, is this proverb true? So let us play it out. A man six feet nine inches tall and weighs 320 pounds is a titan of industry, wealthy and powerful. He makes some bad investments and breaks a few laws. He loses everything and goes to prison for ten years. Now another man, five feet seven, weighs 175 pounds, is a titan of industry, wealthy and powerful. He makes some bad investments and breaks a few laws. He loses everything and goes to prison for ten years. Tell us, which man fell harder?

72. ***Curiosity killed the cat***. This is an old English proverb. It is a warning of the danger of being too curious or inquisitive about things that may be dangerous or none of one's business. The whole proverb says, "Curiosity killed the cat, but satisfaction brought it back." The latter part indicates that even though one might get harmed due to their curious nature, the satisfaction of learning things is worth the risk. It's a head-scratcher, we know. Why curiosity would kill is beyond us. Curiosity used correctly is an outstanding characteristic to possess.

73. ***This is going to hurt me more than it hurts you.*** Have you ever heard of this one before? My, my, my. This one really challenges the imagination. Someone is going to inflict some hurt on you that is going to hurt them more. What? Who would do such a thing to themselves? Who would deliberately inflict harm on themselves? Sounds sadistic to us. And of course, it's *Bulldookey*!

74. ***War.*** What is going on with this one? Why does mankind have such a strong infatuation or, should we say, fascination

with killing one another? This is *Bulldookey* at the highest level. According to historians Will and Ariel Durant, there have been approximately 268 scattered years without war over the past 3,421 years. "War, huh, yeah, what is it good for? Absolutely nothing" (R&B group The Temptations, 1968 protesting the Vietnam War).

75. ***Hatred.*** *Bulldookey!*

76. ***Racism.*** More *Bulldookey!*

77. ***Sexism.*** *Bulldookey, Bulldookey, Bulldookey!*

78. ***I brought you into the world, and I can take you out. Parents who say this to their children.*** Have any of you ever heard of this one? Have any of you ever had this said to you? It is utterly absurd and totally ridiculous. No parent—on the basis of being someone's parent—has the right to murder, kill their child or children. We would think that there would be criminal consequences to such behavior if it were to occur. It makes you wonder how many parents have actually carried out this mandate. How many are in prison, and how many got away with it? As of the writing of this book, the most recent case of a parent carrying out this precept involves Lori Vallow Daybell, who dismembered and buried two of her children in the backyard. She was sentenced to spend the rest of her life in prison.

79. ***Kill the baby in the womb. Okay, kill the baby outside the womb—murder.*** Kill the baby inside the womb is call abortion. Abortion remains a very controversial topic—legal versus illegal. What is not controversial is doing away with the child after it has been born. This is murder. What about when life is forming inside its mother's womb?

80. ***Damned if I do and damned if I don't.*** This is the national anthem or excuse for doing what is wrong. "Damned if I do, damned if I don't" offers that every possible action or inaction would result to a negative outcome and cause trouble. There is no course of action that does not have a drawback. What kind of situation could a person possibly be in where **every choice** available is one that leads to some bad consequence? We believe that some people will always choose the dark side and sing their

national anthem, "Damned if I do, damned if I don't." A truly right-thinking person does not see their decision-making in situations as "damned if I do or damned if I don't" proposition. Example, if I tell the truth, I am damned, and if I lie, I am damned.

81. ***All men are dogs***. What does this even mean? *Bulldookey*! Why are dogs so vilified? An example, "sick as a dog." Why do we pick on the poor dog so much? Why are men bad qualities likened to the dog? Here are a few basic dog characteristics: they are loyal, demonstrate unconditional love, and selflessness. So you tell us, why is the dog, with these wonderful qualities, a symbol of men who behave badly toward women? And if we are using "all men are dogs" as a sexual innuendo, well, women are just as much the dog as men are. Especially using the word ALL. Who came up with this *Bulldookey*?

82. ***The grass is always greener on the other side.*** Something we say that means other people always seem to be in a better situation than us, although they may not be.

83. ***I know you better than you know yourself.*** Parents may be able to say this to their child/children but certainly not an adult to an adult. For adults, if this sentiment is true, then there is something wrong with both individuals—the speaker and the listener. No person should know you better than you know yourself. No person!

84. ***Peace requires us to surrender our illusion of control.*** Whoever made this statement certainly did not understand the true nature of control and perhaps wanted to sound profound. However limited, we possess the ability to manage our lives. This conscious awareness of management is control. Disclaimer exception: people with physical and intellectual disabilities are exempt from this consideration. Now clearly, there are things that are out of our control. One obvious example of this is we do not control the weather. Yet there are many things in our own individual universes we do control. And there are things in our external environments that we control or manage. Some of us simply have something against the word control.

85. ***Maybe happiness isn't what you believe but who you believe***. Phoebe Waller-Bridge, a British actress and producer, is credited with making this statement. It is another head-scratcher. Another classic case of useless profoundness. What if happiness is a state of conscious awareness, a state of being created by emotional and intellectual energy, coupled with exterior stimuli to produce ***I am!*** I am happy. I am not happy. Where does "who" fit in as a dominant contributing factor in your determining what happiness is for you? Perhaps there is a "who" that matters to you, yet certainly your beliefs would contribute more in your understanding of what makes you happy or what happiness is for you.

86. ***You can't teach an old dog new tricks***. The idiom "you can't teach an old dog new tricks" means it is very difficult to teach someone new skills or change someone's habits or character, especially if they are old or used to doing things in a certain way. It is used to express frustration or dissatisfaction when dealing with seniors or people who are resistant to change. The problem with the idiom is one word, "can't." You see, this isn't true at all from the "can't" point of view. You can teach an old dog new tricks. It may be challenging, and it may be difficult, but it can be done. Some old dogs are even eager to learn new tricks as it adds to their portfolio and their repertoire.

87. ***You can lead a horse to the well, but you cannot make him drink***. Definition: this saying essentially means you can show someone something that will benefit him, but you can't force him to accept it. It's all about perspective and perception. People must be properly motivated. If you take the horse out and run him hard, then lead him to the trough where the water is; trust and believe he will drink the water every time. He may drink the trough dry.

88. ***Benevolent deception.*** The notion that it is okay to deceive someone to protect their feelings. What a load of crock. Truth and honesty will trump reasonable dishonesty or benevolent deception every time. Super-duper *Bulldookey!*

89.   ***People who think the far left lane of the highway is "the fast lane."*** This one should not be a controversy, but it is. The prevailing point of view is that the far left lane of the highway is the lane deemed the "fast lane." Talk to your average driver and ask them what is the far left lane of the highway for? You will be told that it is the fast lane. There is no such legal concept in the entire USA. The far left lane on a multilane road is the passing lane, which is used to pass other vehicles. All states have "Keep Right Laws," which require vehicles traveling slower than the normal speed of traffic to travel in the farthest right lane. A growing number of states have designated the far left lane as a "passing only" lane, making it illegal to travel in that lane other than to pass another vehicle. In Texas, for example, there are signs posted on multilane highways that read, "Left Lane For Passing Only," and indicate that the left lane on a highway is not a "fast" lane; it is a passing lane only. After passing someone safely and clearing the vehicle passed, the driver must return back to the right lane. Violation is punishable by a fine of up to $200.

90.   ***LOL.*** Remember when LOL meant "lots of love" and not laugh out loud? For you newcomers who think that LOL stands for "laugh out loud," and it does, it originally stood for "lots of love." So back up because here are a few more newbies for LOL: lots of lag (online gaming), lots of laughs, lots of laughter, lots of Layla, lots of learning, lots of lemons, lots of licking, lots of llamas, lots of lollipops, lots of losers, lots of lube, lots of luck, lots of lust, lots of life, lots of literacy, love on line, love our lord, love out loud.

91.   ***Action speaks louder than words.*** This expression suggests people have a really big problem. Actions should never speak louder than words; they should enjoy the same frequency. Words and actions should be a perfect match. Like in the song "Ebony and Ivory" by Paul McCartney. When they are not in sync, when they are not harmonious, when they are not one, something is amiss.

92. ***Any human who embraces the words nigger, nigga, niggas as a term of endearment***. This piece of *Bulldookey* made the list. But we are not going to spend time on it. Suffice it say, for the folks who support using these terms and for the folks who are against using these terms, the controversy needs to be put to bed. *Bulldookey*!

93. ***All derogatory words that depict human beings***. Except words that are true—such as thief, liar, murderer, lazy, etc.

94. ***Arrogance***. There are those of us who embrace arrogance, confusing it with confidence. But let this record reflect that arrogance is not an attractive characteristic at all. It is an overbearing exaggeration of the importance of oneself. Arrogance is not pretty, good-looking, cute, interesting, exciting, or alluring. Arrogance is pretentious, supercilious, imperious; who wants to be around that?

95. ***Condescend.*** Condescend has the unfortunate characteristic of carrying opposing meanings. There is a positive connotation and a negative connotation. Condescend means, at its first level, to descend voluntarily to the level considered as lower of the person you are dealing with, to be graciously willing to do something regarded as beneath your dignity, deign. At the second level of meaning, condescend means to deal with others in a proud or haughty way. It is in the second understanding of condescend that we tend to give credence to, and it is this element of the word that is frowned upon. Some have referred to this attitude as a person looking down their nose at another as if they were superior. Condescend in this context is closely related to arrogance.

96. ***When hell freezes over.*** People say, "when hell freezes over," to convey the idea that something will never happen.

97. ***Imagination, not intelligence, made us human***. The person credited with this astounding observation was an English humorist, satirist, and author of fantasy novels, especially comical works, Terry Pratchett. If Mr. Pratchett was still living and I had a chance to meet him, I would say to Mr. Pratchett, imag-

ination *is* a product of intelligence. But then again, what do we know?

98. ***Everything's got a moral, if only you can find it***. Another one of those English guys is credited with saying this gem, Lewis Carroll, who authored *Alice's Adventures in Wonderland* and its sequel, *Through the Looking Glass*. He had a knack for word-play, logic, and fantasy. But really, everything's got a moral? As morals deal with the capability of making the distinction between right and wrong, what could possibly make it challenging to find?

99. ***Sick as a dog.*** This common expression dates back to the 1700s. It is used to imply that someone is very sick. In our research, we were not able to determine why the dog was selected to champion this figurative phrase. You could be sick as a chicken, sick as a cat, sick as a frog, sick as a horse, sick as a duck, etc.

100. ***Blind as a bat.*** Let's keep this one short. Bats are not blind!

101. **Thrilled to death.** Death is such a devastating experience for people; why would anyone be thrilled to it? Who is truly excited about dying and joyed over its approach? How about thrilled to life!

102. ***To die for.*** *To Die For* is a 1995 dark comedy, starring Nicole Kidman. But the phrase's meaning—excellence, to be strongly wished for, extremely good, beautiful—is another head-scratcher. What is this twisted fixation with death and dying? When I think of reasons to die for, chocolate cake does not come to mind, a woman's voluptuous body does not come to mind, a very expensive car or home does not come to mind. *Bulldookey*!

103. ***Holding anyone to a higher standard.*** Everyone should be held to the same standard. Honesty is honesty. There are no degrees or different levels of honesty. Trustworthiness is trust-worthiness, loyalty is loyalty, faithfulness is faithfulness, truth is truth, etc., etc. Exactly what is the standard that is higher? We should all be held to the same standard—*the* standard! *The* value! *The* principle! Don't you agree? The baby should learn these standards as he/she develops from the womb onward.

Having more responsibilities or being responsible for more is not the same as being held to a higher standard. *Bulldookey!*

104. ***Expect nothing and appreciate everything.*** My beautiful granddaughter, during a conversation she and I were having, said, "Grandpop, I got some *Bulldookey* for you."

I said, "What you got, sweetheart?"

"Expect nothing and appreciate everything." Her question involved how anyone appreciates anything in life if they have no expectations. Here are some examples: A couple prepare themselves for marriage. Their expectations are to have a family and live a happy prosperous life. Parents send their children to school. The parents' expectations for their children are to do well and succeed. When your expectations are realized, then you can appreciate your efforts. Now of course, there are some among us who have evolved beyond expectations. Yet surely in the ones with higher consciousness, they can discern the importance of expectation in the outworking of planning one's life. The farmer plants seed with the expectation of reaping his harvest. Appreciation is the outcome of the fulfillment of expectation.

105. ***The elephant in the room.*** The fact that an elephant can be in any room and not be noticed is utterly ridiculous! Or that a situation or matter of enormous importance is being overlooked because it makes some of us uncomfortable and is personally, socially, or politically embarrassing, controversial, inflammatory, or dangerous is just downright ridiculous! That this concept is applicable to human behavior speaks volume to how dysfunctional mankind really is. Imagine fifty of the most intelligent of mankind assembled in one room. The unemployment rate for the world is 56 percent. One of those seated in the room is fumbling with his tie, another is looking down at his shoes, three have pulled out their compacts and are looking at themselves in their compact mirrors, others are glancing back and forth furtively attempting to avoid eye contact, another is looking upward at the ceiling. This assortment of behavior goes on for about ten minutes and then someone clears his

throat and says, "I'll address the elephant in the room." Come on, smart people! Come on, intelligent people, get yourselves together. *Bulldookey*!

106. ***Don't shit where you eat.*** This idiom means you should not cause trouble in a place, group, or situation where you regularly find yourself. What is interesting is this, that people tend to start and get themselves into trouble. Why is this? Because of people's propensity to develop trouble, I would prefer starting trouble where I eat as opposed to shitting somewhere else.

107. ***I'll be a monkey's uncle.*** This idiom started as a sarcastic reply to Charles Darwin's theory of evolution. Darwin made the claim that man descended from apes. This was considered ridiculous and offensive because most people believed that man was created by God. It is not clear who originally coined the phrase, "Well, I'll be a monkey's uncle." Nonetheless, it became a popular retort to Darwin's theory.

108. ***You're out of your cotton-picking mind.*** We couldn't get to the bottom of this one. This expression means completely crazy, irrational, or mentally unstable. What is troubling is the "cotton picking." We found no connection to out of your mind to "cotton picking." Its origin probably stems from the days of slavery of Africans in the United States of America, who were used to pick cotton in the Southern states. As such, the idiom has serious racial overtones. *Bulldookey*! And shame on America and anyone who is using this expression for jest. It is not funny!

109. ***No chewing with mouth open.*** As far as I can tell, it is impossible to chew with your mouth fully closed at all times. At some point in the chewing process, you have to open your mouth. I have never seen anyone chew food with their mouths fully open. You? It is very challenging for you to proceed to chew without parting your lips at some point in the chewing process. People who make the effort to chew without opening their mouths at all look ridiculous. Clearly, what works comfortably is mouth open and mouth closed, working in harmony to chew your delicious food! Let's hear a little smacking please!

110. ***Misery loves company.*** This is another one of those expressions that just don't hold up across all mankind. There are certainly times when we are met with some situations that bring our spirit low. And in this state, we might wish to be with someone to be comforted. But is this the case for every conceivable miserable circumstance we find ourselves in? Then there is the perspective that misery wants to be around others to make them miserable too. While some of you may have experienced this episode in your lives, I am glad to report that I have never been in the company of another human being that was miserable, and in that state, their purpose and intentions was to make me miserable too.

111. ***Insanity is doing the same thing over and over again, expecting a different result.*** This principle is attributed to the theoretical physicist Albert Einstein, although it has also been linked to others such as Benjamin Franklin and Mark Twain. This one is troubling for us because from one perspective, it stands up. Yet from another perspective, it falls down. If a person is telling lies over and over again, expecting to just stop one day, maybe we can consider this as insanity, right? Now if a little boy takes his basketball to the basketball court every day and tosses the ball toward the hoop over and over again, expecting the ball to go in and the ball does not go into the hoop, is it insane for him to continue in this apparently futile pursuit? While the actions of the little boy may not be considered in the same light as the liar, it is clear that in both situations there needs to be an adjustment made. But can doing the same thing over and over again gain you a desired result? Doing the same thing over and over again, can it result in a different result? Can your failure, by doing the same thing over and over, turn into your success? This is a very faulty premise. Doing the same thing over and over again can actually result in some benefit to you. A man is trying to date a certain woman. He met her one day impromptu at a restaurant. They exchanged phone numbers. He calls her, no answer. He calls again, no answer. He calls again, no answer. He calls again, same thing, no answer. He

stops calling. Time goes by. Let's say, six months. This woman pops back into his mind; actually she had never left. He picks up his cell phone just as before and calls yet again. She answers the phone! "Hello."

112. ***Larger than life.*** If a person is larger than life, that person attracts a lot of attention because they are more exciting than most people. This is a load of crap. No one is larger than life. When is the last time you took a look at life. It is enormous times one hundred trillion.

113. ***Criminals who say, "Yes, ma'am," and "Good morning."*** Manners are certainly preferable. But with charlatans and criminals' politeness is truly disturbing.

114. ***Double standards.*** This is very bad practice. It creates disharmony, distrust, inequality, suppression of freedom, insecurity, low self-esteem. Another piece of proof of our human dysfunction.

115. ***Do as I say, not as I do.*** The classic position of the hypocrite. This is an example of why we have the expression "actions speak louder than words." We have people saying one thing and doing another.

116. ***When pigs fly.*** Colorful imagery but a total waste of energy. Apparently, we love exaggeration. This expression means that the subject matter in play is never going to happen. A man proposes to a woman, and she replies, "When pigs fly." Too many words. A simple no would suffice way much better and would save time as it would have done away with the confusion caused by "when pigs fly." Do you see the look on his poor face?

117. ***It's raining cats and dogs.*** This is a nonsensical expression used to describe heavy rainfall. Why cats and dogs? Your guess is as good as ours. One possible explanation involves the drainage system on buildings in seventeenth-century Europe, which were very poor and (may have) disgorged the stuff that was in them, including animals that had accumulated in them, during heavy showers. An online rumor circulated through email claimed that, in sixteenth-century Europe, animals could crawl into the thatch of peasants' homes to seek shelter from the ele-

ments and would fall out during heavy rain. However, there is no evidence to support this claim. In its usage, one could say any combination of animals. Any animals you feel fit to choose. It's raining elephants and giraffes; it's raining foxes and chickens, etc., etc., etc. Either way, we personally prefer "it is raining very hard or really hard." Or "it is really coming down."

118. ***Kick the bucket.*** When someone has kicked the bucket, it means they have died. The origin of this idiom is unstable. It could have reference to hanging as a method of execution or suicide, using a bucket to accomplish the feat.

119. ***Sneezing and saying, "God bless you."*** Saying "God bless you" after someone sneezes comes from an ancient belief that sneezing was a sign of illness, death, or losing one's soul. The phrase is attributed to Pope Gregory the Great, who said it during the bubonic plague epidemic of the sixth century. That's how long it has been around. The phrase was meant to protect the sneezer from the devil or to commend them to God's mercy. People used to believe that sneezing caused your soul to be expelled from your body, so "God bless you" or "Bless you" were said as a protection against the devil taking your soul. With all the sneezing we have encountered in our life, there must be a lot of soulless folks walking the earth.

120. ***Pushing up daises***. As with all idioms, this one is supposed to make sense upon examining the context. It means someone has died and is buried under the ground, so therefore, they could be doing some push-ups down there and, in turn, be pushing up the daises. I don't know, I'm shaking my head on this one.

121. ***Putting the cart before the horse.*** Putting the cart before the horse indicates that we are doing things in the wrong order. Here is an example of this given by merriam-webster.com. If you make plans on how to spend money before you have it, you are putting the cart before the horse. Hmmm, we are not so sure about this. I plan on how to spend money I don't have all the time. So when I have it, I am doing the things that I had planned to do with it. I plan to buy a watch. I do not have the

money. I get some money. I spend the money to buy the watch. Win-win, right?

122. ***Rebel without a cause.*** What is this person doing? Get a cause!

123. ***When someone says, "I don't know," when they actually do know***. Another head shaker. The practice of dishonesty and deception are so commonplace these days, it is like it is normal behavior.

124. ***Shit runs downhill***. People at the top of the social or business order don't want to take responsibility for some mishap and find someone below their station to take the fall. This should be a criminal act.

125. ***Fake it till you make it***. I looked at this concept from a mathematical point of view, and I could make no sense of it. The math goes like this: fake it plus fake it equals fake it. Again, fake it plus fake it equals fake it. Again, fake it plus fake it equals fake it. Every time I did the math, I could never get fake it to equal make it.

126. ***Brutal honesty***. What is brutal honesty? There is no such thing as brutal honesty. Honesty is honesty. It is akin to truth. If there is something you have to tell someone and it could cause that person's feelings to be injured, that doesn't make the honesty brutal. What accounts for the brutality of the honesty is the deliverance of the honesty by its host. It is not honesty that is brutal; it is its bestower.

127. ***Tough love***. Really? Tough love? Who is meting out this kind of love? Tough love is defined as the act of treating a person sternly or harshly with the intent of helping them. The fact is, people can adapt to various means of conditioning. Some people are considered hardened and are called hardheaded. For these folks, someone might have reasoned that the only language they can understand is harshness, roughness, and toughness to get through to them. And while these methods may show a measure of success, are these methods absolutely necessary to affect the change desired? Making a child stand in a corner on one leg facing the wall, is this tough love really necessary? Making a man eat dirt until he stops cursing, is this

tough love really necessary? Are these measures truly necessary to alter a person's behavior or attitude?

128. ***Cold as shit***. Here is a head-scratcher. Shit or bowel is actually warm when dispensed from the GI tract. Like anything warm or hot as it is exposed to cool or cold air, it will lose its warmth. This could not occur in warm or hot climates. It would seem that the only appropriate time one could say "cold as shit" would be in cold conditions. You would never say, "That's cold as shit," on a ninety-five-degree day!

129. ***Butter was considered barbaric by the ancient Romans***. Romans participated in a lot of activities that would be found inappropriate today, including gladiators fighting to the death. But they had contempt for eating butter. Eating butter was considered unsophisticated or uncivilized. The term "butter eater" was one of the most hurtful insults of the day.

130. ***Cleopatra VII who ruled Egypt from 51 BCE to 30 BCE***. This historical personage often had her story told by movies made in Hollywood was not Egyptian. She was Greek.

131. ***Christopher Columbus discovered America***. Chris did not discover America. This one is so absurd we put it on the list just for fun.

132. ***R.I.P***. R.I.P. is commonly seen on tombstones of people who have died and have been properly buried. The acronym stands for rest in peace and is used to wish the soul of the deceased person eternal rest and peace. What's interesting about this is that it is not in harmony with the Bible. Ecclesiastes 9:5 states, "For the living know that they will die, but the dead know nothing at all," and verse 6 says, "They no longer have any share in what is done under the sun." This is a wasted sentiment.

133. ***Believing to have someone's back also includes lying for them***. So many people subscribe to this ideology we feel like we need to prepare for war. We don't feel like fighting people who believe that if you are their friend and they need you to lie for them because you are supposed to have their back, that you should be put in the position to lie for them just to prove your friendship or your loyalty. For many, this is an acceptable

behavior. Yet where do we draw the line? How do we become better people? What are our values? Dishonesty, untrustworthiness, deceit, treachery, lying? Relationships are a mess, families are a mess, cities are a mess, countries are a mess. Where do we draw the line to become a better us?

134. ***Don't look a gift horse in the mouth.*** We are told that this proverbial saying means don't be ungrateful when you receive a gift. Now what the horse's mouth has to do with ungratefulness is truly beyond me. There is an explanation on Google if you care to research for yourself. Yet we guess sometimes we receive things that are given an explanation as to what the thing means, and we do not question the explanation. A lot of this colorful use of our abilities borders on the unnecessary. This one is similar to "real men don't cry."

135. ***People who decry crying.*** "What are you crying for?" Have you ever been asked this question? Why crying is perceived as an activity that should not be engaged in is beyond me. It is most healthy. Go on and cry if you feel like it.

136. ***People who claim to not judge, knowing full well that they do.*** Of the many functions we have as human beings, the judge function seems to confuse a lot of people. I think it comes down to this guy named Jesus, who said, "Judge not that you may not be judged" – Matthew 7:1. We think the problem lies in the fact that people do not know the rest of what that guy said. Here it is. "For with the judgment you are judging, you will be judged, and with the measure that you are measuring out, they will measure out to you. Why then do you look at the straw in your brother's eye but not notice the rafter in your own eye? Or how can you say to your brother, 'Allow me to remove the straw from your eye,' when look! A rafter is in your own eye. Hypocrite! First remove the rafter from your own eye, and then you will see clearly (how to judge) how to remove the straw from your brother's eye" – Matthew 7:2-5. You see, it is perfectly all right to judge, but you have to come with the right stuff. This means that people should not be quick to negatively criticize or condemn others because they will be judged

by the same standard. I let everyone know I'm judging! And I continue to work on the removal of the rafter that is in my own eye! I just keep chipping away at it, and I get better in my ability to discern and judge.

137. ***With age comes wisdom***. Another head-scratcher. We could say in a perfect world this would be true. But as things stand now, this is delusional thinking. There are many aging people on this earth and, if observation is to be trusted, are lacking severely in the wisdom department. Developing wisdom through aging is not a natural order of things. Wisdom has to be tried and tested by means of experiences and what we learned from them. Some of us are learning the inherent values life has to teach us, and some of us are not learning at all. This is why the earth's affairs are in shambles. We are lacking collectively in wisdom. The aged and the aging are failing us. Not a pretty picture, we know, but it is true nonetheless. Look around, look around, what do you see? Are all the aged and the aging of the human race demonstrative of wisdom?

138. ***I saw this on Instagram: "I see myself as limitless."*** Talk about being delusional; how is it that this individual does not understand that everything has its limits? Death all by itself sets a limit on our limitlessness. The only being who would have an inkling of what limitlessness is—is who?

139. ***Don't cry over spilt milk***. Once again, my son came to me and said, "Pop, I got another one for you."

And I said, "What you got?"

He said, "Don't cry over spilt milk."

Why not? It seems to us that crying would be in order, especially if all the milk was lost. The thought here is not to be upset over something that cannot be fixed, especially something that is minor or trivial. Well, who determines the degree of importance for another person on what's trivial and minor?

140. ***One monkey don't stop no show***. Are we sure about this? It seems that "One Monkey Don't Stop No Show" is a song recorded in 1950 by R&B group named Stick McGee and His Buddies and was recorded again in 1965 by R&B singer Joe

Tex and recorded again in 1971 by R&B singer Honey Cone, but this version was called "One Money Don't Stop No Show (Part 1)," and again in 1975 (the year my son was born) by country singer Little David Wilkins. I can't speak for you, but I have seen the one monkey stop a whole lot of shows. A few times, I was that monkey.

141. ***Grab the bull by the horns.*** And once again, my son approached and said, "I got another one for you, Pop," and I said, "What you got?" and he said," Grab the bull by the horns." My son said that whatever this is supposed to mean, he is not doing it. On the literal level, it is just too dangerous for everyone to attempt to grab a wild bull by its horns. You might wish to consider getting some training first from someone experienced with grabbing bull's horns. This is the meaning of grabbing the bull by the horns: to approach, confront, or deal with a problem or difficult situation directly with clear and confident action. All of this is fine, but we need a better idiom. Someone is going to get seriously hurt when they grab the bull by the horns.

142. ***According to statistics, African Americans are more likely to…*** My barber who just happens to identify with being an African American told me to be weary of these types of reports. He said there is some *Bulldookey* in these reports somewhere. These reports are very questionable in their accuracy. What do you think? *Bulldookey?*

143. ***No shame to my game.*** Here is a hot one. No shame to my game. This as a concept is debilitating. If your game is on the up and up, why would there be shame in your game? If your game is honest, why would there be shame in your game? Why would a person of integrity make a statement such as "there is no shame in my game" we ask? It seems to me that the only people who could properly use this phrase are those who are indeed actually doing shameful things and attempt to rationalize away the shame by using this phase. For example, an individual who knows that he/she is a habitual liar. This person could say, "There is no shame to my game." Here are

some more examples of folks who might use this phase. The thief who is tearing Walmart up, left, and right. This individual might say, "There is no shame to my game. I'm just trying to survive." How about the married woman or man who are seeing other people and having sex with them. Talking to their friends and telling their friends about their escapades, these folks might say, "There is no shame to my game." Only people who are doing shameful things would justify their actions, their behaviors, using the phrase, "There is no shame to my game." And anyone who thinks that this expression sounds hip and uses it needs to check themselves at the door. This is our humble opinion. *Bulldookey.*

144. ***Time is money.*** No, it is not! Let us say it again, no, it is not! Time is time and money is money. Why man demonstrates a propensity and affinity to deluding himself is beyond me. Who deliberately and intentionally tricks himself. It is like the fig leaves Adam and Eve used to cover their nakedness in the Garden of Eden. *Bulldookey!* We have a fascination with fantasy and fiction. And we have a way of presenting these illusions as if they are really true.

145. ***Life just got real.*** We hear people say this and we cringe. Our whole bodies get tight. What in the world does this even mean? Life just got real. When at any level is life not real? For us, the problem with this expression is the word "just." The use of it suggests that prior to it, "just," there was something else that was not real. Why not just say "things just got serious." Or "this just got serious." But life just got real, hmmm…I just don't know. To us, life is always real.

146. ***Life shows up.*** Another very popular saying of the twenty-first century. Whenever is there a moment in time when life is not present? We have spent hours going back and forth, back and forth, back and forth on this concept, and for the life of us, we cannot locate that moment when life is absent—not present. The need to say it is very problematic from a logical point of view, wouldn't you say? No, you say. You really like this expres-

sion? We know a lot of people like this expression. It is a very popular saying.

147. ***Cat got your tongue.*** This pertains to someone being quiet when they are expected to speak. It was often used in reference to children when they were stubbornly not speaking when asked a question. Instead of a good waste of energy saying, "Cat got your tongue?" why not ask, "Why are you so quiet?" which are five words as opposed to "has the cat got your tongue?" which are six words.

148. ***More than one way to skin the cat.*** Another classic. My father would say this all the time. And I always asked, "How many ways are there, Daddy?" I never received an answer. The phrase means that there are many ways to do something or to achieve a goal. It is often used to suggest that we should be flexible or creative in solving a problem or reaching a destination. The origin of the phrase is unclear and actually has nothing to do with cats.

149. ***Can't piss on me and tell me it's rain.*** The origin of this phrase is obscured somewhere. What does it mean? your guess is as good as ours. Yet here are a couple of examples of its application. Don't excuse what you have just done by saying it is happening everywhere or saying it is not your fault when clearly you are the culprit. Individuals who don't want to take responsibility for their actions are performing devious acts and acting like they don't understand your complaint against them. Notwithstanding, we could think of a lot of better phrases to express this frustration.

150. ***The people who blow their car's horn as soon as the traffic light turns green.*** Have you ever experienced this? You are at the front on the traffic line. The light is red. It turns green and someone immediately honks their car's horn. This is so annoying. Good thing I don't own a pistol.

151. ***It's okay not to be okay.*** I saw this on Facebook. Facebook has a lot of sages pontificating and telling others how to live life. This principle is weak and lacking all the way through. It just doesn't cover all the bases. Its application is wanting. When is it

okay not to be okay? Does it apply to all "not okay" scenarios? We don't think so. First to be considered is okay's meaning. Okay means agreement or acceptance. If you are not okay with someone stealing from you, then it stands to reason that you are not okay with it. So is it okay that you are not okay with the theft? You accept and agree with the theft? If your house burned down, and you lose everything in the house, and you are not okay; in fact, you are sick to your very core; is it okay to be okay with this circumstance? We should never be okay with not-okay situations. If we are experiencing something that is not okay to us, we do not have to pretend we are okay with it by saying, "It's okay." We don't need the other okay to help us manage or cope with what is not okay. We can simply say, "I am not okay," and this should suffice. What we do not need is someone saying to us "It's okay" when we are dealing with a not-okay situation. What do you think? *Bulldookey*? We will let you answer! We hope that reading this did not make you feel not okay, and if it did make you feel not okay, it is not okay. And we apologize! The best we can do when we are not okay is to acknowledge that we are not okay and that we are not okay with being not being okay. Hmmm, makes sense? You tell us.

152. ***Run through a field of tall weeds and you will get pregnant.*** I very rarely use this word, but this is just dumb. Have you heard of it before? My sister-in-law shot this one to me. I searched but I could not find anything on it. She believed it to be an old Southern expression that applied to girls and boys. Apparently, this pregnancy occurs in the act of running through a field of tall weeds. We have no idea how fast you need to run to accomplish the feat.

153. ***Love and God are the two most abused and misused words in all mankind.*** What do you think of having this on the *Bulldookey* list? There has been so much emotional and physical and spiritual damage caused in the name of love. There has been so much emotional, physical, and spiritual damage caused in the name of God. And here is the hit: God nor love are responsible!

154. ***Your beliefs don't make you a better person, your behavior does.*** I saw this post on Facebook. There are a lot of people on Facebook spewing homegrown wisdom. All of them think they have discovered something profound to share with others. Some of it sounds pretty good, we must admit. And some of it is just plain *Bulldookey*, like real men don't cry! Our beliefs shape our behavior. I used to believe I was a good thief, and my behavior bore witness to my belief.

155. ***The (only) person who deserves a special place in your life is someone who never made you feel like you were an option in theirs.*** This is some more Facebook wisdom. Apparently, this individual has an issue with the word "option." So we looked up option in the dictionary. This is what *Webster's Dictionary* said. *Option:* 1) the act of choosing; choice; 2) the power, right, or liberty of choosing; 3) something that is or can be chosen. We will stop here. We see nothing upsetting about being chosen by someone to be in their life. It seems like the perfectly right thing to do. We choose our friends from amidst options. We choose our mates having given consideration to our options. This especially applies to us adults. There are a lot of options and choices to be made in life. We are grateful to those who have optioned us to be in their lives. Now here is the real skinny. You have options too. You have choices too. You don't have to accept the invitation to participate in someone else's life if you don't want to "feel" like an option. Personally, I love feeling like an option and a selection in the lives of the people belonging to my tribe.

156. ***You don't need a reason to help people.*** Facebook again! Listen, even if you help someone just because you felt like it or you help them just because, this is your reason. It amazes me how some people misapply or misunderstand meaning. I did it "just because" is a reason. On Facebook, there are hundreds, thousands of people asking for help. They want you to Cash App them money. Or they want you to send them gift cards. These folks' anthem is "You don't need a reason to help someone." We do need a reason to help someone. In fact, we need

reason. Period. Our faculty for reason is innate and is coded in our DNA.

157. ***If you don't take risks, nothing will change***. So we went back to *Webster's Dictionary*. Risk means the chance of injury, damage, or loss, dangerous chance, hazard. Obviously, you don't **need** to put yourself at risk to affect change in all situations in life. Some change may be achieved without having to put yourself in danger or in a position to experience injury emotionally, physically, or spiritually. I guess how one sees these things is based on individual perspective and perception and are situational. The problem here is wording and meaning. And the word causing the concern is "nothing." Plenty of things can change with efforts that do not put oneself in danger or a hazardous situation.

158. ***Do not ever apologize for the madness which made you a warrior.*** What does this even mean? Madness? Back to *Webster's Dictionary*; madness means dementia, insanity, lunacy. Examples of these kinds of situations or circumstances are not within my wheelhouse. I tremble to consider their possibilities. Warrior? Back to *Webster's Dictionary*. Warrior means a person taking part or experienced in conflict, especially war. There are a lot of combative people on this earth. There are aggressive nations on our planet. But whatever the conditions are, that accounts for this concept, they absolutely need to be apologized for. Perhaps even forgiven.

159. ***Great things take time. Be patient. Never give up.*** Listen, everyone, everything takes time. Whatever amount of time is needed to attain greatness, it takes time. One hour, one day, one month, one year, ten years? Understanding the preciousness of your existence, your life, is greatness enough.

160. ***Sometimes it takes me all day to get nothing done.*** I must admit, I struggle with the "nothing." So I went back to *Webster's Dictionary*. Here is how nothing is defined: no thing, not anything, naught, no part, nonexistence, nothingness, a thing that does not exist. Then there was a slight shift in meaning, something of little or no value or importance. Stop! Something of lit-

tle or no value ought not possibly mean the same thing as nothing. It adulterates the meaning on nothingness and changes it to something small and insignificant. No wonder people are confused. They can't possibly be the same thing. *Bulldookey.* The thing of little importance or of little value cannot be considered as nothing. It is something! In fact, imagining nothing takes quite the effort. Try to actually do nothing. You can't do it. Laziness is something; idleness is something. When we are sleeping, we are doing something, and while we sleep, our bodies are working. I often wonder about the answer "nothing" given sometimes to the question, "What are you doing?"

161. ***People who don't appreciate complaining.*** There are reasons why we complain. Here is the meaning of complaint: 1) express dissatisfaction or annoyance about something; 2) state that one is suffering from pain or other symptom of illness. The energy we use to complain is perfectly normal to us. Have you ever heard the question, "What are you complaining about?" followed by, "You should be grateful." It is a head-scratcher. When we have a legitimate grievance, it should be voiced. The complaint is a powerful tool. Complaining is how we get things done, get things moving along. Why there is a lack of appreciation for complaining is beyond us. We love a good complaint because we understand the "human condition." It is screwed up! It is a horrific mess!

162. ***No one stays with you permanently. So learn to survive alone.*** Even if this concept is referencing death, the ultimate departure from life, to "learn to survive alone" is just a ridiculous and tragic point of view. First in order to accomplish learning to survive alone, one would have to be alone. Not everyone has a family. I have met people who, according to them, have no family. They were an only child. Their parents were only children. They have no aunts, no uncles, no cousins. Their grandparents are deceased. This is a very tough reality, we would imagine. Then what about friends? We know people who have been friends from as early as five years old, who continue to be friends and are now well along in the stream of time. It begs

the question: What is going on with the individual who feels and thinks like the only recourse in traversing life is to "learn to survive alone" and proceeds to advise others to do the same? This approach doesn't seem healthy. There are currently over seven billion people living on earth, why go it alone?

163. ***The long story short.*** Watch out for the long story short. Sometimes the presenter forgets that they said, "long story short." The long story short becomes the short story long!

164. ***Do you want everyone to like you?*** When I was case managing for Catholic Charities, I would ask this question to the program's participants. The answers I received were utterly amazing from the participants. I would always, before asking this question, say, "Listen to the question very carefully." I was always amazed with the first answer I would receive. It seemed like it never changed. The first person responding to the question would say, "Everyone is not going to like you." Or the first person responding would say, "No, I don't want everyone to like me." Crazy, right? Then one day, a young participant in the program asked me, "What is your answer to the question?" It was the first time a participant had asked the question *to* me. And here is the answer I gave, "Yes!" I told that group of men on that day, "Yes, I want everyone to like me." I told them that I liked myself, and because I like me, it only made sense that I would want all others of mankind to like me too. Whether everyone I meet and know like me or not, the question speaks to what I want. And I certainly want everyone to like me. Why? Because I adore me! And it makes no sense at all to me that others, all others, would not adore me too! The contrary responses to this question truly demonstrate a dysfunctional mental, social, and spiritual condition common in people. What the hell is the problem? What do you think the world and life would be like if all its occupants truly liked themselves, truly adored themselves, truly loved themselves? With all this going on, where would be the room for dislike?

165. ***Vibrating or shaking your leg up and down.*** This apparent nervous activity is frowned upon by some and is considered a

major distraction. Whenever I am shaking or vibrating my leg, I enjoy doing so. I certainly don't think of it as an activity that would or should disturb others. Why should my leg shaking serve as a distraction to anyone? Why are people frowning their faces at me? Leg shaking is comforting and soothing. It also helps with time management.

166. ***Chopsticks placed in the center of a bowl of rice.*** In my other occupation, providing transportation via Lyft and Uber platforms, I asked my rider of Chinese descent to give me some cultural *Bulldookey*. I asked this individual for her input because she knew me. I had given her a ride before, and she remembered me. She said, "I know you. You wrote a book. You gave me a bookmark designed as your book. And you are working on a second book called *Bulldookey*." Well, I was blown away. Thinking about *Bulldookey*, I asked her to share, if she could, an example of *Bulldookey* from her Chinese culture. She pondered for a moment or five. When she spoke, she told me about chopsticks sticking upright in food, especially rice. It is considered a curse in her culture because it reminds people of incense used at funerals and is considered to bring bad luck. Keep in mind that this young woman of Oriental descent was young. She was not old. She was twenty-three years old. When I asked for a tidbit of *Bulldookey* from her culture, she served up the taboo nature of placing chopsticks upright in rice. I do believe she offered this information with the utmost respect.

167. ***Don't touch the head of the Buddha or monks' statue.*** The same young woman of Oriental decent also offered this gem. It is considered disrespectful to touch the head of the Buddha statue. She said that this rule also applied to statues of monks.

168. ***Young people of Chinese descent cannot pick up their chopsticks to eat until all the old people eating have done so.*** This, too, came from the same young Chinese woman. All the children seated at the table for breakfast, lunch, and dinner must sit and watch their elders reach and get their eating utensils before they can reach for theirs. This is some conditioning, but we all have been through it as children. And then we practice

these same ghastly rituals we were given as children when we become adults. But some of us break away to freedom. Case in point, the next item of the *Bulldookey* list.

169. ***Can't drink your beverage until after you have eaten all your food.*** This piece of gold nugget came from a female Lyft rider who is Jamaican. We also had this custom in my household… laugh out loud! This Jamaican woman told me that she taught this dining etiquette to her children and that she still practices this until this day. She revealed to me that she has a nineteen-year-old daughter who has rebelled. She said she used to argue with her daughter, but now she just leaves her alone. The child broke away to freedom. How many of you experienced this as a household custom growing up? I used to want to grab that tall glass of iced tea so badly, and I would look at my parents, and I knew I would proceed at my own risk.

170. ***This is going to be a short story.*** I had young woman in my vehicle who was an Iraqi. She was thirty-five. I shared with her that I am writing a book called *Bulldookey*, and I explained that *Bulldookey* is a synonym for bullshit. She smiled and said that she understood. I then asked her if she would share with me examples of *Bulldookey* from her culture. What she related to me sounded like a horror story. I told her that I thought she was beautiful. Not the world-class beauty, but the subtle beauty that is in the eyes, the cheekbones, the mouth. She started her story by telling me how beauty is viewed in her country. She spoke of women of unquestioned beauty having facelifts and cosmetic alterations to their faces. She said that it's mainly the beautiful young girls of her country who are doing this, and she could not comprehend why they did not cherish their natural beauty, why these young women did not appreciate the beauty they were born with. The frustration of this fact weighed heavy on her face. She then began to talk about how women are treated in Iraq. To explain this, she spoke of her marriage to a man who treated her extremely disrespectfully and was mean and harsh. She could not go anywhere without his approval. She could do nothing without his approval. Her money was lit-

erally her husband's money. She said the laws, the government of her country, did nothing to protect the women from the atrocities of the menfolk. I wanted to know how she got here to America. She said that she was a refugee. She had to escape for her life. She also said that she loves it here in America because here in America, she, as a woman, has freedom.

171. ***Any law that protects a sitting or ex-president from facing criminal charges when they have committed a crime.*** What say you?

172. ***If it's not broke, don't fix it.*** Yes, if it is not broken, don't fix it. But just because a thing isn't broken, does not mean it cannot be improved. In the creation of this book, we had sentences that were grammatically correct. Yet we sort ways to improve them. These sentences were not broken, but they could use improvement. So we sort to improve them. Sometimes we want things to remain as they are. A person has had the same curtains at the windows for ten years; they are old and dusty. They won't change them because they are not broken. They like them a lot. Just because something isn't broken doesn't mean that it does not or cannot use improvement.

173. ***Be the bigger person.*** One of the riders on one of the transportation platforms, Lyft or Uber, offered this one. So I put it on the list. When I asked why was being the bigger person *Bulldookey*, she simply said, "Because it is." It seems that the individual who is always sacrificing, bending over backward, turning the other cheek, walking away from the fight or quarrel reaches a point where they don't see the benefit of their efforts. It seems that being the bigger person at the time does not have good rewards.

174. ***Watching paint dry.*** People think that watching paint dry is boring. I beg to differ. It is one of the most exciting experiences you can ever have. I mean, you spend the amount of time painting whatever it is you are painting and then you are finished. Now what? You watch that baby dry, and you can't wait to touch it.

175. ***I am not a product of my circumstances. I am a product of my decisions.*** The person who offered this gem of wisdom obviously did not know the meaning of circumstance. So back to *Webster's Dictionary* we went. *Circumstance:* 1) A fact or event accompanying another, either incidentally or as an essential condition or determining factor; 2) any happening or fact: event; 3) conditions surrounding and affecting a person. So it becomes clear that we are products of both concepts: decisions and circumstances!

176. ***If you don't see the value of having me by your side, I won't convince you.*** Question: If you are not demonstrating your value in a convincing manner, how am I to see it? Am I supposed to just look at you and see that you are a loving, thoughtful, caring, open-minded, trustworthy, honest, generous human being? Don't we all have to demonstrate who we are and continue to demonstrate who we are every day of our lives? Aren't we to continue to improve ourselves, grow, and mature every day? Why would I stop trying to convince you of my value when this is a fluid process? Everything, all our efforts, are for proving, for demonstrating consciously and subconsciously who and what we are. I, for one, love this dynamic process of life. Even the continuation of proving and convincing myself what my value is and what my values are. I just told a lie the other day. Oops!

177. ***The truth doesn't need support.*** I had a niece who would say this all the time. She had an affinity for not telling the truth. I have heard others say, "truth needs no support." This is hardcore *Bulldookey*! The truth is the truth needs all the support it can muster. Let us give you an example of the truth needing all the support it can get. If the truth needs no support, explain to us what is going on in the following example: You are accused of crime. You stand before the court of justice and the judge, and you plead not guilty. You say, "I did not do it." This is the truth. You are innocent. A trial date is set for your case. Why? The trial date is set for you to demonstrate with proof that you are innocent. And even then, banking on "truth doesn't need

support," you may fail to prove that you are indeed innocent. It is a conundrum, I know. The truth is under attack every single day. And it needs truth warriors to defend it. What say you?

178. ***Broke-ass, begging-ass people on Facebook, telling others how to live life and how to gain wealth and prosperity!*** If you are on Facebook, you know what I am talking about. Someone sends you a friend request. You check out their page. They seem cool. They have all kinds of inspiring quotes and advice from relationships to finances. You accept their friend request. Very, very, very soon thereafter, this time period fluctuates; they send you a message, stating, "I need your help." The help that is needed is always money! Ridiculous, just ridiculous! *Bulldookey* with two thumbs up!

179. ***You don't know a woman until you understand what she's not saying to you.*** I saw this on Facebook. Do you understand it, whether you are a man or woman? I have been married. I have three children. I am a grandfather and a great-grandfather. Two of my children are women. I have had a few relationships in my lifetime. I did not learn that to know the women I shared my life with, I needed to understand the things they were not saying to me. That is not to say that by using my female intuition that I received from my mother, I couldn't discern the unspoken nuances of the women in my life. The open communication we shared was more than sufficient for learning and getting to know one another. We highly recommend open communication. The woman might not have a man who is tuned with intuition. And the man might not have a woman who is in touch with female intuition. So open communication it is. You won't go wrong, trust us!

180. ***Old keys won't open new doors.*** Perspective and perception on display once again. I am going to go old school on this one. There once lived a man who lived over two thousand years ago, who spoke of some keys. He called the keys, keys of the kingdom. Well, those keys are very old now, and yet they are continuing to open new doors. Perhaps this saying works in the physical realm. But it loses its power in the spiritual realm.

181. ***The scariest place to be is the same place as last year.*** I don't remember who gave me this outrageous gem. Oh, that's right, Facebook again. There are a lot of scary things in life, wouldn't you agree? I don't know that being in the same place I was in the last year qualifies as one of them. What on earth does this expression even mean? Some of us were in very good places last year. Are we scared that this year, we will still be in that same place? We think it is criminal to say something with no explanation or clarity. We could really harm someone.

182. ***The world is full of nice people. If you can't find one, be one.*** We have no doubt that the contributor of this wisdom really thought they had come up with something truly profound to say. It is an eyeball scratcher all right. How is the world full of nice people, and you are unable to find one? Are you living in the wrong part of the world? Are you even in the world? Are there no nice people in your family? None of your schoolmates, neighbors, coworkers, nobody you know is a nice person? If this is indeed the case, it is an extraordinary phenomenon. Then how does one become a nice person? How do you *be one*? Isn't all learning the same? Whatever it is that you are, you had to learn. You learned how to count, learned to dance, learned to write, learned to talk, you learned to cook, etc. How does one learn to *be* nice if there is no one available for them to learn from? We don't know about you, but we are stupefied beyond comprehension with this concept.

183. ***Don't take this personally or it's business, not personal.*** Example, "Don't take this personally, you are fired." Another example: Someone has intercourse with your spouse. You confront them, and they say, "It wasn't personal. I have nothing against you." We are not going any further with this nonsense. If anything affects you in any way or manner, it is personal. If you witness a brutal car accident and watching it horrifies you, the effect of the accident is personal to you, though you yourself were not involved in the accident. No one can determine for you how you are affected by the events and circumstances you encounter in your life.

184. ***God won't put on you more than you can bear.*** This is another one of those biblical texts that has been reworded and misconstrued over the centuries. It is a miscue on 1 Corinthians 10:13. It reads, "No temptation has come upon you except what is common to men (all people). But God is faithful, and he will not let you be tempted beyond what you can bear." The experiences we have in life that involve temptation is what is being discussed in this scripture. It is not about the house burning down, or your nation going to war, and you getting drafted. This scripture is not about you being in a car accident and breaking both your legs and arms and your rehab is brutal. No, the writer makes it clear that what he is referring to are things that are "common" to men.

You see a horse unattended. You look around, searching to see if anyone is watching. You want the horse. The urge is hot, strong, very intense. To take this horse, you know it is wrong. You fight the urge. From somewhere, you find the strength to walk away.

You are married. Someone is flirting with you. They are pleasant to look at and funny. Their flattery is like butter in the hot sun. You think of your spouse. You are feeling unwanted emotions that feel good. The voice is asking you to go with them. Your head is swimming; you are teetering. You hear a distant sound calling your name. For the moment, you are safe.

There is a test being given at school. You are not well prepared. The student sitting next to you is one of the smartest in the class. The class is called to order, and the test commenced. You are nervous, knowing you could fail this test, and your parents will be extremely disappointed. You feel the urge to look on the page of the student sitting next to you. You move your eyes toward the direction of this student's paper. You think that you can be successful, not failing the test, if you could just see this student's answers. It is not easy. You strain your eyes to see the student's paper. You hear a voice inside your head. It says, "Stop it."

There are many multitudes of such examples of temptations like these that are common to men. We will not bore you with an exhaustive list. We believe that you get the picture. The principle of God not putting upon you more than you can bear has been distorted, contaminated, and misused.

185. ***When you are going through the storm, someone says to you, "That's par for the course."*** My beautiful, lovely, and intelligent daughter-in-law said to me, "Daddy, I got some *Bulldookey* for you."

I said, "Finally, what you got?" Finally, because I had been asking her for some slice of *Bulldookey* for this book from the book's inception.

And she finally gave us this wonderful gem. When we are faced with some adversity, she called the storm, and someone says to us, "That's par for the course."

Her thought is this: this is the last thing on earth she wants to hear when she is facing tough, extremely challenging circumstances or situations in life. And she is correct. Par for the course means what is normal or expected in any given situation. "What is normal" being the key ingredient here. Going through the storm certainly cannot be classified as normal. No, the storm is exceptional, not the normal affair of life. What say you?

Bulldookey is author Millard Edward Streeter's second literary effort. His first entry is titled *Restored to Sanity, God, Christianity, and NA.*

Mr. Streeter wanted to give the world a lighter fare, a piece of work that people could just have fun with. He hopes that he has accomplished this with his presentation of *Bulldookey.*

Pamela Elizabeth Smith was born and raised in Queens, New York. *Bulldookey* is Ms. Smith's first literary effort. She and her coauthor came up with the concept of *Bulldookey* while chinwagging on the phone and simply could not stop laughing. She is eagerly anticipating the production of her next entry for your enjoyment.